PRAISE FOR THE EXTRAORDINARY WORK
OF TONY BURROUGHS

Get What You W
The Art of Making and Manifest

"The principles and practice of Conscious Intent... ...u Manifestation that Tony Burroughs and the Intenders of The Highest Good have "downloaded" from a Higher Source, developed, and set forth in this book, will transform and elevate every aspect of your daily life in the most magical and amazing way, while inspiring and guiding your Soul to rise to Its Highest Calling!"
—*Maria Muldaur, multi-Grammy-nominated*
singer, producer and environmental advocate

The Code: Ten Intentions for a Better World

"Tony Burroughs has done it again... *The Code* is a masterfully written book of pure inspiration. It is a priceless guide to help us all reconnect to our spiritual humanity. Through his ten practical intentions, Tony has produced *divine scripture* for the new millennium. *The Code* is by far one of the most important books of the 21st century!"
—*Dannion and Kathryn Brinkley,* The Secrets of the Light

The Intenders Handbook:
A Guide to the Intention Process and the Conscious Community

"We are using the Intenders Circle process and seeing amazing things happen. This is the practical application alluded to in *The Secret* and is the rest of the process you are looking for..."
—*Dan Hunter, Humanity's Team Texas State Coordinator*

The Law of Agreement

"An awesome book! Tony is a shining gift to the world. He directs you to raise your consciousness, sign a new contractual agreement with yourself, stand in your power, and be the best you that you can be. Follow the call for manifestation and freedom. Journey beyond your own magnificence in this fabulous classic. Well done, Tony!"

—*Yvonne Oswald,*
award-winning author of Every Word Has Power

The Vision Alignment Project
(with 2 Million Alignments and counting!)

"Thank you for the *Vision Alignment Project*...I think you are making one of the most powerful differences—if not *the* most powerful difference on the planet today."

—*Marianne Friend, United Kingdom*

The Intenders Bridge Messages

"Thank you so much for these 44 steps. They could be sold at Tiffany's as the most precious jewels from the purest crystal."

—*Jean-Claude Vanden Plas, Bruges, Belgium*

"I'm so excited! For weeks, to everyone in earshot, I've been raving about *The Intenders Bridge* online series—and even more recently about the Intenders books I've been reading."

—*Jane Sibbett, Los Angeles, CA*

Also by Tony Burroughs

Books/Nonfiction

Get What You Want: The Art of Making and Manifesting Your Intentions

The Intenders Handbook: A Guide to the Intention Process and Conscious Community

The Highest Light Teachings

The Law of Agreement

The Code: 10 Intentions for a Better World

I See a World: The Best of the Vision Alignment Project

WINS: Manifestation Stories from the Intenders

Fiction

The Code 2: The Reunion: A Parable for Peace

The Intenders of the Highest Good: An Adventure Novel

DVDs and CDs

The Intention Process: A Guide for Conscious Manifestation and Community Making

On the Road with the Code (2-DVD or 3-CD Set)

Living by Manifesting (3-DVD or 3-CD Set)

All Books, CDs, and DVDs are available
at www.intenders.com and www.highestlighthouse.com.

what
you need
to know
now

what you need to know now

The Lee Ching Messages

by
Tony Burroughs

Published in the United States by Viva Editions, an imprint of Start Midnight, LLC, 101 Hudson Street, Thirty-seventh Floor, Suite 3705, Jersey City, New Jersey 07302.

Printed in the United States.
Cover design: Scott Idleman/Blink
Cover photograph: TK
Text design: Frank Wiedemann
First Edition.
10 9 8 7 6 5 4 3 2 1

Trade paper ISBN: 978-1-63228-035-0
E-book ISBN: 978-1-63228-036-7

Library of Congress Cataloging-in-Publication Data is available on file.

*This book is dedicated to the Highest Good
and to all who work without wavering on Its behalf.*

TABLE OF CONTENTS

Gratitudes

It's been my great honor to be the scribe for Lee Ching for the last decade. He has helped me on countless occasions through my good friend, Tina Stober, and he has blessed me directly with the information in my books, *The Code*, *The Intenders Bridge*, and *The Vision Alignment Project* Visions. My gratitude overflows for the gentle, loving guidance he shared with me, and that I share with you now in these positive, encouraging messages. *The Lee Ching Messages* have helped me see that there is more to life than what we've been led to believe, that peace and fulfillment on all levels are ours for the creating, and that a better world is on its way to everyone who lives and breathes on this amazing planet.

Tony Burroughs
July 2015

A Helpful Note

This is a bibliomancy book, a tried and true oracle for the twenty-first century. You can open it to any page and it will tell you what you need to know in the moment.

In fact, without further ado, let's test it. Go ahead. Right now. Suspend your disbelief, silently call in the Highest Good, and open this book to any page. The message you get is the message you need.

You'll see...

Introduction

The first Intenders Circle was made up of my friends Mark, Tina and Betsy, and me. We'd been meeting together on Sunday evenings for about a month when, surprisingly, Mark announced that Tina had a gift; she was a messenger. I immediately looked over at Tina and asked her what he meant by that. As she humbly explained, she had been a part of a forward-thinking group back in the '80s just outside San Diego called *Love in Action*, where people gathered every week to hear her "bring through" a highly evolved, ascended master by the name of Lee Ching. For those who are unfamiliar with Lee Ching, he has had many lifetimes on this Earth but is not incarnated here at this time. He's been a Taoist Immortal in China, a commander in chief of armies in Lemuria (the civilization that preceded Atlantis), and is the male archetype of mercy. Like his female counterpart Kuan Yin, the archetype of compassion, Lee Ching has vowed to keep returning to this planet until humanity's suffering is finished forever.

Well, Tina's gift was news to me. I'd known Mark and Tina for many years, having met them when they lived across the street from my mother in Kailua-Kona, Hawaii. We spent many days together at flea markets or selling our various wares by the side of the road (I was in the Bali import biz, and they sold adjustable-waist, Velcro-belted pants), and during all that time Tina never mentioned anything about her "gift." As it happened, we all moved from Kona and lost track of one another—until one day when we met again on the windward side of the Big Island near Hilo.

So when Tina mentioned Lee Ching, I said that the most exciting thing I'd been doing lately was sitting in the rainforest watching the guava trees grow. If she was willing, I'd like to talk to Lee Ching. The rest, as they say, is history. From my very first meeting with Lee Ching, I knew I was in the presence of the most loving, caring Being I'd ever met. Over the next several years (until I left Hawaii to take these wondrous Intenders teachings out to the world), we held spiritual guidance sessions at the end of our weekly Intenders Circles, and I asked Lee Ching every question I could think of—all of which he answered with such wisdom, grace, and accuracy that we never wanted these sessions together to end.

Needless to say, our small circle of four grew rapidly, and, on one particular evening, Lee Ching told us that he was not exclusive to Tina—that he would "come through" me as well (now you know where my books come from). Not only that, he said he was willing to help others in our circle who also wanted to become messengers—and so it wasn't long before

Betsy was bringing through Mother Mary, Lois was bringing through White Buffalo Calf Woman, Alva was bringing through Madame Pele, et cetera. By the time I left Hawaii for California, the room was packed every Sunday night with people wanting to take part in our Intenders Circle, as well as to listen to the panel of messengers in our accompanying spiritual guidance sessions.

From our point of view, the information we received during this magical time was profound. It was way ahead of its time. In fact, we were told by our guides that it was being given to us well before the time when humanity would need it most—and when it would have its greatest impact on the peoples of the Earth. Clearly, what with all the changes we are going through almost daily, that time is now.

The Lee Ching Messages come from the transcripts of our early Intenders spiritual guidance sessions, as well as from those of us who have done our best to integrate this wisdom into our lives since then. These gems were given to us in the Spirit of service and helpfulness, which is the same Spirit with which we offer them to you. It is our intention that you use them to help yourself through this time of great transition, to reach your highest calling in life, and to bring forth the experience of Oneness unto all who abide on this beautiful Earth.

Chapter 1

POWER WISDOM

Your world needs you now. These times of great change call upon all those who are holding the light to set an example for others by being happy and uplifted regardless of the circumstances around them. Remember that your inner poise need not be swayed by outer orchestrations, and that the mainstream consensus reality is but one reality out of an infinite number of realities you can choose to place your attention on. It is wise for you to take part in the realities that serve you and discard the ones that do not, and, in that way, instead of commiserating or becoming sorrowful, you will remain happy and shining your light for all those around you to see.

—LEE CHING

"Tony, you're going to write books and make movies," Lee Ching said in one of the very first spiritual guidance sessions that followed our Intenders Circles. Anyone who wanted to stay after we finished saying our intentions and gratitudes was welcome to visit with him for thirty minutes at that time.

"No way! No possible way!" I announced stubbornly. Back in those days I was a bit rougher around the edges than I am today.

He just looked lovingly into my eyes and then spoke the two words I was to become so familiar with over the next twenty years. "*You'll see,*" he said, smiling so sweetly.

Ten books and five websites later, here I am, still amazed at what happened with the widespread popularity of our Intenders information and the words of Lee Ching that came true. Yes, I was skeptical at first; however, it didn't take long before I began looking forward to these guidance sessions each week. In fact, his words and phrases were touching me so deeply that I began writing them down and collecting them into a file I called Power Wisdom. Perhaps, I thought, one day someone else will find them as helpful and prophetic as I do.

Here is one of the early Power Wisdom gems Lee Ching shared with us:

At this very moment you are creating with your thoughts,
with your words, with your actions.
You are constantly creating
the world around you.

At the time he said this, I really wasn't sure what it meant. All I knew was that it resonated deeply within me. It wasn't until several years later that that I was able to incorporate this beautiful piece of information into my daily life.

Who you think you are
is only a very small part
of who you really are.

*What you're looking for
is what you're looking with.*

*Everything you need in life
is always shown to you.
Your next step is always unveiled before you.*

*It will come to pass
that you will have a thought
and it will be there.*

Oftentimes things may be happening all around you
that seem to be discordant, and you cannot imagine
what is going on. But you must remain focused
and steadfast and be able to see through
and not get caught up in the mundane dramas
that are constantly being perpetuated on this planet.

The real revolution is in consciousness.

*All of the dramas on Earth are nothing but a play
that is taking us to our awakening.*

How silly it was that we thought
we were something less than amazing,
that we were less than immortal.
We've never been less than anything.

The body will pass, but the soul never does.

You're creating the world you're going to enter.

You're becoming something more than a human being.
You're becoming a Universal Being.

*You have to believe that when something good comes to you
that all good things can come from it.*

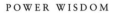

Keep one foot in the Heavens and one foot in the world.

People are getting ready to become
the Godly Beings that they are.

Once you're awakened to a certain level,
you can't go back.

There is no death.
Those who have left are still here.

What causes people to give up
is that they think they can't make a difference.

There are parts of you
who are exploring other realms all the time.
The more you go toward those realms, the happier you'll be
because it's lining you up with your soul.

The media has nothing to do with helping you advance in life.
It's only producing crime, sorrow, sickness and unhappiness.

It's the lie that's got to die.
The real you cannot die.

Everybody is getting what they want.
It may not look like it, but it's true.

That's why human beings are here—
to live their lives freely and fully.

Know that you are assisting others
by your own realizations.
You then enhance and increase the possibilities
for others to go where you have been.

Your desires come from that which moves you forward.

Self-empowerment—
the ability to easily manifest that which we desire—
is available to all for the asking.

The light that shines within you
when you are waking up in the morning—
intend that that light show out to the world
and that it be a magnet for goodness and kindness
and gentleness and all good things.

One needs to first experience peace
in order to understand it.

*You are being taken to places
where you are needed.*

You are powerful beyond measure.
This is what is being rediscovered at this time.

Your opportunities have been drawn
into your experience by you.
They come to you because you believe they will come to you.

You get what you say you want
and you get what you say you don't want.

You're here for a reason.
You put yourself here.

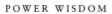

Good things can happen in unexpected ways.

Your words and your thoughts
are more powerful than you may know.

Your purpose is to be revealed to you
so that you can spread your wings
and cover this Earth
with that which is your creation.

You are moving toward the light
and you are bringing the light back to the Earth.

Who you think you are can change.

The ground you walk on is sacred ground.

That which we do to one
we do to All.

*What you learn mostly from enlightenment
is the acceptance of everything that is—
instead of living in the world by your rules
and expecting everyone and everything
to line up with your rules.*

*You are so much more
than you think you are.
You are the answer to the prayers of God.*

*Nature will never allow the tyrants
to continue indefinitely.*

*Truly, you are moving toward something
much greater than your desires.*

Spirit is ready to do whatever is necessary.

*Remember: your purpose here on Earth
is to evolve to your highest possible state of being.*

The source of your supply is so immense.
It's all there for you
just waiting for you to tap into it.

Much has been hidden that is now being revealed.

Always ask for and intend to have your freedom.

It'll all come together.
Just smile and watch it all come together.

The world is different than you've been led to believe.

Remember that there is no past.
Everything begins anew in each moment.

Let not your heart be troubled.
You will open up to that which is awaiting you,
as you are awaiting upon it.

It all comes from the same Source.

There is loving, uplifting light
available to you at all times.

There is no wrongdoing—
only lessons that take us to a greater awareness.

Eternity is much longer than most people think.

*A perception change is in order
so that you can accept that which is already yours.*

All things are moving toward
that which you are moving toward.

*Life is a journey, and in allowing information
to come to the surface,
oftentimes you have to let it come up
in the course of life itself.
Life is a process.
It is not a timeline that begins at our birth
and ends at our death.*

Chapter 2:

ABUNDANCE AND GRATITUDE

Be open. You are here to receive. But first, in order for you to be fully open to receiving and experiencing your financial well-being, as well as your inner well-being, you must tune in to your own gratitude and be grateful for whatever it is that you already have in your life. Remember your gifts. When you give freely of your gifts, you will be highly rewarded in every way imaginable. Then, all you have to do is ask for what you want, be open for what you deserve, and be a willing and ready receiver for the highest of gifts. Gifts from the Universe. Magical and miraculous gifts...

—LEE CHING

Elko, Nevada, is a lonely little gambling town I've ended up in many times over the years as I crisscrossed the country showing people how to set up Intenders Circles of their own. On one occasion I'd been called there to talk to a group of fifty people—but only six showed up! I'd driven a thousand miles with barely enough money to get there, and after the event was over I was back in my motel room, looking out the window, brooding because so few had attended. The venue was in a smoke-filled casino with huge portraits of mean-looking gunslingers on the walls (not the typical comfy living room I was accustomed to), and I had a long drive ahead of me back to the coast. Needless to say, I was frustrated.

That's when the phone rang and it was Tina saying that Lee Ching wanted to talk with me. I said, "Great!" because I knew he often seemed to sense when I needed help and was unable to find it in myself. So after Tina and I got caught up with the goings-on in our personal lives she stepped aside and Lee Ching came in. This is part of what he said to me:

That which is meant to be yours will come to you. Just as those of you who are aligned with the Highest Good will eventually experience your highest ideal, so shall your daily needs be met. You need never worry about your survival because there was a special mechanism put into place long ago which regulates and guarantees that everything you need will be there for you in the exact moment that you need it.

Oftentimes it will not appear until the instant before it is needed, but you may be assured that, while you are waiting, you are being strengthened. As you learn to trust in this wondrous process, the obstacles and hardships of life fall by the wayside and are replaced by a serenity that knows no limit. These times of great upheaval are truly gifts unto you. You are constantly surrounded by an environment that is conducive for bringing out your most fulfilling form of expression. Your ego, the part of you that is in service to yourself, is giving way to a much larger, grander you—the you that is in service to others. You are blossoming in all your glory, and it is this blossoming that you have always longed for. Be open, be available, and, in the meantime, be at peace. Your prayers and intentions are all being answered.

The next morning as I drove alone across the hot Nevada desert I received a call from a lady who was an Intenderpreneur in southern Florida. She thanked me kindly for the support my work had given her and then gifted me with the second largest donation I'd ever received—$2,500. After hanging up the phone, I pulled the van over to the side of the road and shouted out with joy!

Looking back at it all, that's when I stepped into my greatest abundance. I learned that as long as I'm living my calling by doing what I came here to do, and I'm lined up with the Highest Good, I needn't ever be concerned about anything. Whatever I needed, including money, would always be there for me.

*The abundance and prosperity that you are seeking
is already there waiting to pour itself upon you.*

There is infinite abundance already present.
However, by your thoughts, your words and your deeds—
and by your actual stressing and being uptight over it—
you are using up the very energy needed
for the breakthrough so that it can flow to you.

*At this time, in this age we are living in,
there is still a medium of exchange known as money.
This will change, but, at this time, you can use it
and be open to it and allow it to flow through you.
Do not hold on to it or store it up,
but be a channel for it to flow through you.*

You have to be willing to receive help and abundance from wherever it comes.

If you are counting your blessings every day,
and are in gratitude for your gifts,
you will receive more and more
than you could ever imagine.

Be open to receiving
at least as much as you are giving—
because other people need
to have the experience of being the giver.
If no one is willing to receive,
then how can other people be givers
and have the growth
that comes with learning to give?

Fear not to ask and gifts will be given.

You are not to get something from people—
you are to give something so they will expand.

That which you give out
is also that which you get back in return.

Take care of it so it can take care of you.

*Abundance is having enough to spare
and enough to share.*

It always helps to know when to recharge.

It's your small self that keeps you from living in your glory.

Can you imagine what it will be like
when we care for each other,
when everyone is helping everyone else,
when everyone has whatever they need—
their food, their shelter, and more...

Your rewards come from not giving up and not giving in.

Money and fame are not really the judging factors of success.
That's the ego at work.
Most people are looking outside themselves
to measure their success,
but success and joy are an inside job.

Consciousness is huge—
bigger than the sky,
bigger than all of space.

It's all about how you feel when you help another person.

Every time you have a negative thought about money,
you're sabotaging yourself.
Total abundance is there for everyone.

It's important to let people know
how much you appreciate what they do for you—
even if it is the tiniest thing—
because all the things people do for you are gifts.

If you help other people
and trust that, in the helping,
you'll be helped,
you will.

Giving and receiving are one and the same.
It is not possible to give without receiving.

Accept that which comes to you—
even if it is not in the form you expected.

Your needs are always met.

Though you have asked for that which you desired,
there is so much more that is awaiting to be given to you.

The good Earth has so much to teach you—
if you have ears to hear, eyes to see, and hands to touch...

Sometimes your abundance is only waiting
upon your appreciation and your recognition of it.

*Our environment, in all its wondrous manifestations,
has the potential for great change.
It is alive and ready, at a moment's notice,
to respond to our direction and work with us
to co-create purity, beauty and abundance beyond measure.*

It's all free to begin with.

It's okay to make a lot of money,
but it is important not to let your imagination
run away with you.

The Earth is a live entity
and it responds to you as you respond to it.

As soon as you see things in a new way,
with a perspective of gratitude
and an opportunity for growth,
you will be rewarded immensely.

Chapter 3:

SELF-MANAGEMENT

You become those you are invoking. These times call upon you to surrender, to let go—of not only your attachments to things, but also your attachments to your current identity, to who you think you are. Holding on to your smaller self, with its name, its earthly identifications and its encumbrances will keep your higher self at bay. However, as you let go of your current identity and begin to call on the higher beings—the masters, angels, wise elders, and great archetypes—you will experience your true glory and the grandeur of the best life has to offer. For, as these great beings come inside you, they become you. And, gradually, you begin to realize that you have become them.

—LEE CHING

Some people love living in the big cities, but I've always been a country boy who likes gardening and nature. For me, there's a freedom—an expansion—that comes from living out of town with lots of trees and green around. This kind of environment not only allows me to be more creative, but it also lets me digest any of the heavy, dramatic situations that come into my life every so often.

I recall one instance in 2004 in central California when I was helping my good friend Adrian make her transition. Adrian had three daughters whose lives were so busy that they could only visit their mother every few days. However, on this particular day, all three were gathered, arguing and backbiting over little things while their mother lay there in bed dying. Since I was living there and caregiving for Adrian, I couldn't help but get involved in their dramas to some degree. At a certain point in the afternoon I'd finally had enough and I went to my room, closed the door behind me, said a prayer/intention, and in came Lee Ching. I wrote down what he told me as fast as I could.

In order for you to see things from a higher ground, you must learn to detach from suffering and drama. The faster you can learn to do whatever it takes to lift yourself up and out of dramatic situations, the better it will be for you and for all those around you. If you need to go out the door and shut it behind you and say, "I'm not going back there for a day or two," then do that. If you're in a situation at work where you're feeling really drained and you need to regenerate, go out into Nature. Nature is there for you. It is filled with vital life and energy. Avail yourself of it. It is your birthright, as a human being, to be with the trees, the wind, the sun and the rain. These things add unto you. They regenerate you. They recreate you.

When Lee Ching took his leave, with Adrian's three daughters still emotionally involved with one another in the living room, I went out, got in my old Volvo and drove to the ocean. As I began walking the sands of Grover Beach, I felt Lee Ching coming in again with another download—and that's when he gave me *The Code: Ten Intentions for a Better World,* the best tool for daily living and self-management I've ever seen.

What you think about all day long
is what you manifest in life.
It's the Law.

You can intend to be shown what your next step is.

Create peace in yourself
and it will spread out from there.

How do you nurture the growing light?
You keep believing it will continue to grow.

Your values are expanding.
Put the important things at the top of the list.

You who are a seeker of truth
must ask questions.
What if? Am I? Am I not?
These are the tools you use
as you wade through worlds
of illusion and deception,
seeking answers where others are complacent,
resolution where others are confused,
peace where others are conflicted.

*It is good to experience uncertainty
and it is good to experience certainty.
They are both very high spiritual qualities
and yet they appear to be opposite.*

Things can come to you at the last minute.
In fact, you know that you are learning patience
when things are coming to you at the last minute.

To be in balance,
cultivate moderation in all things.

Share your fears
and lose them in the telling.

You need not be concerned about the future...
only the Now.

You are doing it to yourself.
No one else is doing it to you.

You can ask a question as you are falling asleep
and wake up with the answer.

If people simply lined up with their Higher Self every day—
before they let catastrophe in—
this world would be brand new.

Your next step is always given to you.
Be open. Be expectant.

*Spend more time looking within
rather than looking without.*

You can have a direct experience
with your guides
by going within.

Everyday, ask God:
"How can I help? Who can I help?"

Lining up with our Higher Self—
that's the next step for each of us and all of us.

Self-empowerment comes not from the ego,
but from our Higher Self.

Check in with your Higher Self.
Your Higher Self sees further.

*The thinking mind thinks it knows
what is for our Highest Good.
But this isn't so because it is so affected
by societal and cultural beliefs.*

People who want to do better, do better.

*Ask for help from your Higher Self
and, step by step, you will be shown.*

*People need people
who are coming from a calm,
reserved, meditative state
to help them.*

When you come from your Higher Self,
there is no effort.

Really busy people aren't any happier.

People have a tendency to build up
a cloud of regrets or guilts, or beliefs
that they are undeserving, or they're not enough,
or of things they think they should have done differently.
These things keep them from seeing the light.

They can't control you if you don't let them.

Only when you know that you don't know;
that's when you can begin to learn.

*Sometimes it's best for us
to get away from things for a while.*

Knowing in your heart and soul
—with every cell of your being—
that you are in the right place at the right time
—and feeling grateful and blessed for being
in the right place at the right time—
will help you dissipate your fears.

*It's always wise to combine
that which is helpful to others
with that which is enjoyable to ourselves.*

It is only ourselves that sometimes get in the way.

*If you're driving down a country road
and you see flowers,
and your neighbor is driving down the same road
and sees only weeds, who is right?
What you're tuned in to, you create.*

*If you perceive yourself to be a victim
you are giving others the power
to take energy from you.*

If you find your harmony in doing nothing,
then do that.

Freedom has been forgotten.
That is why it's important to spend time outdoors.

It is time for the feminine side
to stand up
and be in balance
with that which is its masculine counterpart.

*Sometimes you have so many talents and gifts,
and if you are not using them or giving them out,
they get all stuck inside you.*

Feel freer to go into Nature when you need to.

When people are born into this world,
they have chosen to do certain things
before they come here—
and sometimes, because of free will,
they change their mind.

If one refuses to use his willpower,
his apathy wins out.

Having a belief system
is better than having no belief system.

Confusion is another kind of resistance—
because when you are scattered
you are not moving forward.

Adversity strengthens us.
Who could we learn more from
than our own brothers and sisters?

If you create peace within yourself
and harmony in your home,
they will move outward
into the world at large from there.

Chapter 4:

SUPERCHARGE YOUR INTENDING

What if you only believed that your life is filled with magic and miracles and that is all that can happen to you? What if, before any thoughts of fear or lack came in, you started out your day with that intention—that only magic and miracles are coming to you? Everything in your life would get better.

—LEE CHING

We've seen it happen over and over again in our Intenders Circles. Someone will come to the Circle with a burning drama and need to vent. In the early days, we didn't let people go into their dramas because it seemed to drain some of the energy out of our Circle. Things worked better if we just kept to saying our intentions and gratitudes.

On occasion, however, when the Circle was smaller and we had time for Intenders to express themselves more fully, we learned to let them go into the drama for a bit—not long enough to wallow in it, but just enough so we could get the gist of what they were experiencing. Then we'd ask them an all-important question: *"What's your intention around all of that?"*

What we found is that after people made an intention around the drama, they typically felt better right away—and they would come back to the Circle a week or two later, and guess what? No more drama, because the intention they made in the Circle had manifested for them.

Here's the way Lee Ching put it:

If someone is stuck in their drama,
steer them to making an intention around the drama.
Pretty soon, their intention will manifest
and there won't be a drama anymore.

*What you are reaching toward
is also reaching out toward you.*

What you are looking to create
is a positive, happy life—
and the more you intend
that your thoughts are positive and happy,
the more that is what you will create.

It is wise to get proficient at manifesting—
at getting that which you desire to come to you
as easily and effortlessly as possible.

*There is a direct relationship
between making an intention
and the manifestation of it.*

Those who get up in the morning
and provide a direction to their day
by saying their intentions, their affirmations or their prayers
have an entirely different experience than those who do not.
Everything comes easier.
Their lives run smoother.
They get the things that they desire.

*It's a good idea to intend
that you are always guided, guarded, and protected.*

Your desires are in you to be fulfilled.

You can make intentions
until you're blue in the face,
but if you have no belief structure behind them,
they will not work.

Your intentions are always received.

*You can intend that you be shown the best project
to put your highest intentions into.*

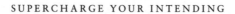

Always be simple and to the point.

*For some people, the biggest challenge
to becoming proficient at manifesting
is remembering to make their intentions.*

*We don't dwell on how or when
our intentions will manifest for us;
we just know that they will.*

You can manifest anything and everything that you need—
if you believe that you can.

The timing of your manifestations
is what's frustrating for many.
Our Higher Self doesn't operate off of ego.
It operates on Universal Timing,
and this is where acceptance comes in.
There is an order to the Universe
and we have to accept that order.

All your prayers and intentions really affect the whole.
That's why humanity is starting to withdraw from war
after centuries of time.

You can intend that everything
needing to be known is known.

What you say is what you get.

*So often human beings sabotage themselves
by not trusting that the Universe
will bring their creations to them in the perfect timing.
The "Knower" is willing to wait until the last minute
for his or her intentions to manifest.
The "Novice" is not.*

Say your intentions everyday.

*Practice using unbending intent
and unending gratitude.*

~ The Five Easy Steps ~

1. Test the Intention Process and be open.
2. Get your first "win" and acknowledge that it works
by expressing your gratitude.
3. Develop your trust by practicing
and getting more "wins."
4. Notice that your trust turns into a "knowing"
that you can manifest anything you desire.
5. Have fun, stay filled with gratitude,
and always remember the Highest Good.

Keep moving forward and be open to receive.

It's not the vision itself—
It's the intention behind it.

It is for each and every one of your desires to be fulfilled, because that is what brings you to the state of desirelessness.

It always works.
Whether it works to your benefit
or your detriment is up to you.

*Intention is so fluid
that sometimes people forget
to acknowledge that they received it.
But if they intended it, they will receive it.*

Intend for what is honestly in your heart.

*Emblazon three little letters
upon your consciousness—A S K.*

Expressing gratitude is the Intention Process
having come full circle.
It starts out with making an intention;
then you see the manifestation of it;
then you express your gratitude for it.

All the things you seek are just waiting
upon you to open the door.
All you need do is ask.

A circle of people is like a jewel box.
Place your intentions in it.

Everything in your world—
the world at large
as well as your individual world,
including everything you see,
hear, smell, taste, touch, and feel—
is the result of a thought manifestation.

*You can intend
that you have all the resources you need at all times
so that you are fulfilling your calling
while you are here on this beautiful, abundant Earth.*

Chapter 5:

REFINING YOUR VISIONS

*There is an unprecedented awakening occurring,
and more awakening will come out of each person
reaching out for something higher and knowing
that there is more than the mundane life to be lived
on this planet. There can truly be a paradise on
Earth and you are bringing it into existence by your
believing in it, intending it, and envisioning it.*

—LEE CHING

Lee Ching awakened me from a sound sleep in the middle of
the night on the Summer Solstice. At the time I was living in
my small RV at Richard Blackstone's place on the Willamette
River just outside of Eugene, Oregon. I immediately sat up and
grabbed a pencil and notepad from the bedside table.

"It's been a couple of years," he began, "since you wrote
the Ninth Intent of The Code—*Share Your Vision.* Don't you
think it's time for you to share some of your own Visions?"

I wondered what he was up to. He didn't usually wake me
up at dark-thirty. "What if you began writing Visions for your
ideal world and shared them with your readers? What if you

picked topics that interest you and wrote short Visions, two or three paragraphs each, and put them out to the world?"

It sounded like a good idea to me, even in my half-asleep, half-awake state. I was in limbo at the time, having recently finished *The Law of Agreement,* and was waiting to see what my next project would be. "How do I start?" I asked him.

"Set up a new website, call it 'The Vision Project' or something similar, and begin uploading your Visions to it. I'll help with the writing. Make it free—and arrange it so your readers can line up with your Visions so that your Visions become their Visions, too." He went on to say that it would be a way for them, by aligning with my Visions, to make a difference in the world. "So many people," he said, "don't feel like they can make a difference in your world, so you'll be providing them with a vehicle for expanding their horizons. They'll begin to see that your world doesn't have to be the way the newspeople say it is. It can be better, so much better. By sharing your Visions, you'll give people renewed hope. They'll flock to your new site. *You'll see!"*

Early the next morning, I told Richard about Lee Ching's middle-of-the-night message, and we both began writing Visions right away. Now, over four hundred Visions and two million Alignments later *The Vision Alignment Project* is raising the spirits of people from every country on the Earth by showing them how good it can be for all of us.

The time will come, in our very near future,
when one more person envisions a peaceful world
and, with that seemingly tiny action,
the scales are tipped.
The storm clouds disappear and a new world—
the world that we deserve to live in as our right of birth—
opens up before us.
It will be like a miracle...but it's not really a miracle.
It's only us having changed our thoughts.

Picture the end result from the very beginning.

You can create your life
to be any way you want it.

We are all expanding.
Some people hear things coming;
some people see things in Visions or pictures;
and some people just feel it.

Your thoughts come first,
then your experiences.

I intend that, from this moment forward,
you and I and all of the people
we come in contact with,
and all of the people they come in contact with,
and all of the people they contact
—until it fills the entire Earth—
live in utter joy and peace.

You can create a world
that is always in support of you.

So what would you like your Vision to be for your world?
Would you like it to be scary and dramatic,
or would you like it to be peaceful and lush
and filled with fruits of all kinds?

*Always be moving toward the ideal
instead of looking at things
that get in the way of it.*

*You are really beginning to realize
that the world can be as you envision it.*

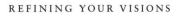

Happy endings are always a good thing.

The reality that you create is up to you.

Do a Vision for your own life every day.

Ask yourself:
"What's the best thing that can come out of all this?"

Step into your own Vision for yourself.

The more you envision what's possible,
the more it becomes reality.

You are bringing your Visions to life.

Thought precedes everything.

You can have it.
You can have it all.
You've just got to believe that you can.

*Visualize yourself in any place
where learning will occur,
and you will be there.*

Peace is truly possible in our lifetime!

Know that you can create your reality
in each and every moment.

*There are enough resources
on the planet right now
for the whole world to be fed and cared for.*

*You deserve to have the kind of setting
that really charges you up,
that makes you feel at your best.
You deserve the kind of setting
that supports you.*

This is what conscious living is all about.
It is about being aware
of the infinite number of choices
available to you
in any given present moment situation.

How much greater you are
than you think you are.

It can keep getting better and better.

When we have peace,
the Masters will return.

Just imagine it!
It can all be free.

Peace is just a thought away.

Whatever we're putting our attention on,
that's what we are becoming.

Everything is possible!

You have a Vision within you
of what you know yourself to be.
Stick with that Vision. Go toward that Vision.
Make that Vision more alive.
That is what you came here to do.

Chapter 6:

RIGHT ACTION

It helps to take notice of your subject matter and to understand that when you are talking about something negative, something that you wouldn't want to manifest in a million years, it moves closer to manifesting simply by the act of discussing it. Whatever you talk about—whether it's positive or negative, something you want or something you don't—is on its way to you.

—LEE CHING

I remember driving out of Albuquerque having just broken up with my girlfriend of three years. I was in tears and wondering what had just happened. One day we were deeply in love, and the next day it had all gone sour. I was heartbroken.

Somewhere outside of Gallup, my cell phone rang. It was Lee Ching and he knew exactly what I was going through. Before I even started into my rant, he told me that my guides in my soul family pulled me out of New Mexico because, if they hadn't intervened, my girlfriend and I would have gotten back together—and I would have stayed in Albuquerque. He said I had to go to California because my destiny awaited me there. People were waiting for me in California, and the red carpet would be rolled out for me when I got there.

Of course, I squawked, and he said, *"You'll see!"* Then he continued, saying that we all have a path that we set for ourselves before we come into this life on Earth, and we need to stay on it if we want to continue to grow spiritually. My path, he said, was to write more books and be open to travel to help people set up empowering communities, communities that would be needed when the paradigm of peace came in. I have a big calling, he said, and I had to stay on it if I was going to evolve to my highest state of being. Besides that, he said (with a smile in his voice), I'd have more fun than I could ever imagine in California.

When I set the phone down, I felt much better. Good things awaited me. Driving across the border into Arizona, I was out of my funk and back on my path, looking forward to whatever was next.

You have known before you came here
that there would be a time when you would be called upon.
The time which you have been awaiting has come.
It is time for you to follow Spirit without hesitation,
and to live in the light on a daily basis.

Oh, by the way—that red carpet *was* rolled out for me in California. I lived on mountaintops in Escondido, Topanga Canyon and the Mount Shasta area, met my new publisher in Berkeley, set up dozens of Intenders Circles all over the state, and made so many new friends I couldn't count them all. Lee Ching was right again.

Think—
if you could be doing
what it is that makes you the most happy.
Then go and do it.

When you harm anyone or anything
you are only harming yourself.

When you step into your calling,
all things open up for you,
and the way is made clear for you to do
that which you have come here to do.

When something is happening
that is uncomfortable
and not much fun for you,
it is important to look for the gift in it.
Look for the gift and you will find it.

*Start with yourself
and then start to move out into the world,
and the world will receive you with open arms.*

You must be willing
to see life from a higher place.

Bring out the good in others.

Whether someone is labeled as a valiant soldier
or a ruthless criminal
depends on whose side you're on.

When you're thinking
that someone else is going to attack you,
you are actually helping to create that attack.
A defensive position always invites an attack.

When we realize that we are becoming
exactly like those we oppose,
shouldn't that be reason enough
for us to stop opposing them?

*Sometimes you need to grow
into that which you've already created.*

*When you put your energy
and your will behind it,
you get results.*

*Is what you are thinking about or talking about
what you want to be manifesting?*

Everybody is affected by you when you are your joyful self.

*Once people realize
that they're the ones
who created the mess in their life,
they'll begin to straighten it out.*

Don't close off to possibilities.

*If people aren't going toward their purpose in life,
there is no reason for many to keep going.*

*The way to go into the next level of Being
is to live it now.*

If everyone would just stop
and tune in to what their purpose is—
to what they're doing here—
everything would clear up
politically, economically, and personally in a jiffy.

*What's more important than anything
is to take care of everyone.*

When you're tuning in to Universal Truth,
you're One with everything and everyone.

The awakened person acts,
while the unawakened person reacts.
Reacting gets you nowhere.
Continue to fight with the boogieman,
and you're reacting.
Don't react to what seems to be going on out there.

Keep acting,
and not reacting to every little thing
that everyone would like you to react to.

You'll always be shown the right direction.
You just have to trust in it.
You'll go, "Oh, if I go this way, it leads to more suffering,
and if I go that way, it'll be fun."

*Your heart's desire is fulfilled
when you help another person.*

Western culture has trained people
to be wary of helping others;
to be wary of being of service.
It's trained people to care only for me, me, me.
But that's the very thing that takes away
your drive and your feeling for others.

You can clean and cleanse your life
so that you are walking around in sublime bliss.

When you are near a Spiritual place, go there.
These are places of ceremony
where people came together
and unified in the past.
You can tap into that energy,
even if it is centuries old,
and you can use it.

*The TV news and commercials
are suggesting sickness, poverty, aggression and so forth.
So why don't you suggest that that is what is being done?*

Why keep patching up the old
when the best use of your energy
is to envision the new?

Mercy lets others go free.

See the Essence of Divinity in every person.

Once you stop using the animals as a food source,
they will begin to recognize that you mean them no harm,
and they will open up to you.

Misfortune is always accompanied
by an incredible gift.
Look for the gift and you will find it.

Keep asking; keep opening; keep finding.
Make it a quest.

*It is more important to see the actions
than to listen to the words.*

It is for yourself that you see others in their highest light.

Speak freely and know safety.

Instead of seeing anything as a problem,
see everything as an opportunity.

If you are in a situation
that doesn't feel good to you,
you don't need to remain in that space.
Just be clear not to imagine it
into something bigger than it is.

*Harming another will never
give you the results you truly desire.*

Do what you know in your heart is best at the moment.

Be not afraid to speak your word
—whatever it may be—
for the service of others
and the service of mankind as a whole.

Be gentle to all living creatures.

What if all of us were seeing everyone,
including ourselves, in our highest light?

As you are living your life fully and freely,
happily and healthfully, inspired every day,
you are an example to others that it is possible.

Chapter 7:

LOVE AND HEALING

The veils between the dimensions are getting thinner, and soon they will be lifted entirely. A doorway, or an opening, is presenting itself—and it is the end of the world as we know it because we, the beings on the Earth, are changing. We're getting in touch with deep issues and clearing them very rapidly now, and this is creating a new perception of being One with everything and everyone. We're changing into new people on a new Earth, and the only way to enter the new experience is to love everyone unconditionally. Unconditional love is the new paradigm, for when you love everyone unconditionally, there is no way you can harm anyone or anything. You can only be love.

—LEE CHING

Magic and miracles pervaded the house in Leilani. Our Intenders Circle there produced so many amazing manifestations that, in turn, produced so much gratitude. Each week, the house was filled to the brim with new Intenders wanting to live their dreams and take in the wisdom that poured forth from our spiritual guidance sessions.

It was in the Leilani house that Lee Ching taught Betsy how to bring through Mother Mary, and Betsy was a natural; she was as clear as any spiritual messenger I'd ever met. She already had it in her when Lee Ching sparked her—and to our surprise, she was considerably more animated than we expected, sometimes getting up and walking around the room, which was magical in itself because Betsy's eyes were plastic, prosthetic devices. She hadn't seen since the age of two.

One night, with a roomful of people, Mother Mary was coming through Betsy and she got up and walked across the floor to a lady named Theresa, who had blue veins in one leg. Betsy/Mary knelt down before Theresa and placed her hands on the painful leg, and, within moments, Theresa's pain was gone. Mother Mary then looked up at Theresa and said, "You are healed here this day—and as long as you believe that you are healed, you will be. You needn't look anywhere but inside yourself for confirmation that you are well, now and forevermore. Go now and be at peace."

Theresa walked out of the house that night a well woman. We all saw it. In fact, we even visited her at her home the following week and she was fine. The week after that, however, to our great dismay, she felt a twinge in her leg and decided to go back to the doctor. He reconfirmed her original diagnosis—and immediately Theresa's painful issues returned.

In subsequent guidance sessions, both Lee Ching and Mother Mary said that if Theresa had been stronger in her belief that she was healed and had not bought into the doctor's beliefs, she would have remained well and pain-free from the time Mary touched her.

It wasn't long after that when Lee Ching came through me and said:

You can shed light into the darkness.
You must be willing to say to your friend,
"I see the perfection in you,
and I know you have the ability to fight this thing off,
or to dissipate this thing that is affecting you."
You must see the light for others
if they are not seeing it for themselves.
This is how you help each other.
If one of you is feeling ill,
the other one who is feeling well can see the wellness,
so that you are always holding the template for wellness
and projecting wellness toward one another.

When we give a name to somebody's
sickness, we are giving power unto it.
We remind ourselves that our words have power,
and when we speak the name of any disease
—whether we think it is our own or someone else's—
we are actually reinforcing and feeding the disease.

*It isn't necessary for you to prove
how wonderful you are to other people,
because you are already wonderful.*

*If a friend of yours is telling you how sick they are
and all that's wrong with them,
always see them in their perfection.
If you add to their illness by your belief in it,
you are not doing them any good.*

Perfect health is available to you at this time.

Create with love
and your creation will love you back.

Be open to all opportunities,
because sometimes they come
in different packages
than you are expecting.

*Our challenges are there
in order to lead us to a greater awareness.*

You've never done anything wrong.

You will go through periods in your life
when you will simply follow Spirit without hesitation
and let It lead you each and every day of your life
to your greatest joy—because it always will.
That is the perfection in all things.

*You need not go to the level of suffering
in order to help others.*

You can always ask your angels to talk with their angels.

Your body has the ability to heal itself.

You are beautiful just as you are.

*More people on this planet die of boredom
than anything else.*

The only way to enter the new experience
is to love everyone unconditionally.

What people have been doing with their heads,
they're going to start doing with their hearts.

You have to be able to converse
with people who are in a bind.

If you're stuck in your thinking,
when you start to help other people
you'll start to feel again.

*When you become your Higher Self,
you fall in love with yourself.*

Help people to move forward.

Support life in every thought you have.
Support life with every word you speak.

If calamity befalls us, it is okay.
We're ready, without complaint.
This is the posture that strengthens our immune system.

Laughing clears and cleans your emotions.

Turn your anger into passion.
That is the next step.
Take notice of it and transform it into something useful—
not something that will lash back at you later on.

Sometimes all a person needs is for you to listen to them.

By your thought shall you be well.

Resolve anger with the joy of existence.

Purging of the body is a good thing.
Sometimes an illness is a purging of the system
that is giving you more immunity
and making you stronger
against the effects of toxic substances
you may have come into contact with.

WHAT YOU NEED TO KNOW NOW

*Possibly because of an illness or a shock,
some people are all of a sudden
awakened to their higher purpose.*

298

Prayer and fasting
can change almost any situation
in just a few short days.

Many of you will be involved in healing in many ways:
healing the Earth, healing each other,
healing people you don't even know.

Love yourself—you deserve it.

Let nothing come between you and your joy.

It is not wise to destroy that which takes care of you.

It is the job of your angels to help you.
But they can't if you don't ask.

The same energy you use to heal others,
you can use to heal your planet.

In order to heal another, we must:
1. Be compassionate
2. Have their permission
3. Invoke the healing power of God or The Highest Good
4. Stay grounded
5. See them in their highest light.

Sometimes the lesson is not your lesson.
Sometimes you are a participant
with someone else who is learning a lesson.

The Earth is needing attention.
It is needing Love.

Grace is the greatest gift,
and all you need do is ask for it.

Go more into the quiet.
Quiet is where the Universal Sound is heard.
It has a way of raising your body to heal itself.

There is no shortage of people to love.

Everyone is a healer,
and healing begins in thought.

Be good to one another.

Be aware of that which you embrace.
Those who embrace scarcity shall be subjected to it;
those who embrace sickness shall experience it;
those who embrace violence shall perish by it;
and those who embrace love in the fullest
shall be embraced by it in return.

We can choose emotional excitement,
or we can choose peace.
Forgiveness will bring us peace.

Allow healing to occur,
no matter where it comes from.

Go forth with love
and all is added unto you.

Chapter 8:

AN INSIDE JOB

Joy is an inside job. But if you never stop, you can't find it. If you're in the material world all the time every day, you're really not advancing. It's in the stopping of all the busyness that people find their happiness and their true joy. Really busy people aren't any happier because they don't have the time. They're trapped in the material world, and that world just keeps piling on more material for them to deal with.

On the other hand, when you are practicing being present in your daily life and in meditation— even for a short time each day—you're going to other levels: heavenly levels. There are parts of you that are exploring other realms all the time, and the more you go toward those realms, the happier you'll be, because you are aligning with your Higher Self. Windows and doors are opening right now for those of you who are going into the silence that is within you.

—LEE CHING

Lee Ching always told us that it's all an inside job, that we are projecting our world outward from inside of us, and that our projection is the illusion while our inner world is what's permanent and real.

Hardly a spiritual guidance session went by without him suggesting that we spend time in meditation every day, because therein lies the gateway to other realms and all that we longed for. He said that once we are able to hold our attention on any one thing long enough, worlds within worlds will open up to us. In fact, over the years, he used many different ways of reminding us to quiet our minds. Here's one of the more colorful ones:

> *Oftentimes our mind is like the barker at a carnival, yelling, "Come one, come all! Come every thought imaginable. Step right up and I will view you. I will give you energy and attention!" even though we know, deep down, that everything we put our attention on gets stronger.*
>
> *Whenever our thoughts are flying here and there, it is up to us to ground our thinking. We need to let our thoughts know that we're in charge. We can tell them, "Get behind me! Leave me be! I have no use for you! You are only holding me back! I have an opportunity in this life to be a God/Man, to become master of my fate. I will not listen to you one minute longer. I will no longer be swayed by your trickiness!"*

If you are trying to move forward, you are only trying.
You are not moving forward.
If you feel that you need guidance, go within.
Don't look somewhere else or for someone else
to give you what you know is already inside of you.

The mind will run you around,
lifetime after lifetime,
until you still it.

Peace is not just a word. It is a way of being—
and when you experience it within yourself,
in your meditations,
you are assisting others in the world
to have that peace as well.

If you are feeling fear and recognize it,
you have the choice of using
the other half of your thought,
which is your positive thought.
Your positive thoughts
are always available to you
in all situations.

*It is good to be open
to that which is coming to you from within.*

If you want rapid acceleration,
spend time with yourself every day in silence.
Listen to the sounds and look for the light.
It's that simple.

How can you hear the truth from within
if you are never silent?

*No book, no movie, no ceremony, no device
can take the place of spending time inside yourself.*

Anyone who has practiced meditation
for any length of time will tell you that it is cumulative—
that it just gets better and better.

*Every single one of us
is capable of bringing through our higher self.*

Your joy, your comfort, and your security
all come from inside of you.

*If you want to go quickly
to that which is your Higher Self,
recreate yourself every single day
through meditation and being in Nature.*

In your meditation,
keep looking between your eyes and higher.
There you will see it.

The path is to go within, to listen,
to allow the next thing to show itself to you.

The truth lies in the spaces between the mind chatter.

*More important than the science of mind
is the silence of mind.*

When you experience God's presence within,
you perceive the Kingdom of Heaven without.

*It is important that those with good intentions
override those with bad intentions—
and those with good intentions
override the bad intentions within themselves.*

*Meditation is a clearing process
that is opening and awakening you to a higher power.*

No chemical ever enlightens the way quiet meditation can.

*To make a connection
with the Knower inside of you—
you do this simply by asking.*

Let your thoughts know that you are in charge.

The Native American teachers are returning.
They speak to you through your reading
and in the stillness of your mind.
Sometimes they even speak to you
through the rocks, the animals, the trees, or the wind.

You must have faith
that the answers are there within you at all times.

You are your attention.

You must have your listening time
in your meditation
as well as your petitioning time.

Listen to your intuition
and you will be where you need to be
when you need to be there.

If you are in touch with your ancestors
or your loved ones,
you will be given the red-carpet treatment,
and you will find your way,
and you will know exactly where you are going.

If you meditate every day,
you begin to perceive other dimensions.

*Look within
and see what would give you the most joy.*

*Go with the blessings from all of your own guides
and teachers and masters within,
for that is truly where you will find them:
within you.*

Chapter 9:

THE HIGHEST GOOD

Oneness is the true calling for all Beings. Walk through that doorway—into the Oneness, into the Light. Have the pure intention of everyone awakening to the Highest Good. That should be the intention that is in the minds of everyone, in the words of everyone, and in the hearts of everyone everywhere.

—LEE CHING

We always felt that it's important to call forth the Highest Good. We've watched many people over the years make intentions, but it never felt right to us if they left the Highest Good out of the picture. After all, why would anyone want to manifest anything if it wasn't for his or her Highest Good? It didn't make any sense to us, and that's why we always followed our intentions by saying something like, *"In order for our intentions to manifest, they must serve the Highest Good of the Universe, ourselves, and everyone concerned."* Lee Ching taught us this phrase in one of our very first Intenders Circles and it resonated to the core with us. He then went on to elaborate, saying:

When you are always asking
for the highest and best good,
that is all that can be delivered to you.

That little bit of information changed all of our lives...

*We always intend that in order for our intentions to come to us,
they must serve the Highest and Best Good
of the Universe, ourselves, and all others.*

You are learning that once you intend something,
and it is in your highest and best good,
it will make itself available to you.
If, however, you are still believing
in fear or suffering
more than you believe in the Highest Good,
you will be experiencing more of that.

When you're intending for the Highest Good,
you can turn any area into an area of light, love, and beauty
NOW.

You are God in manifestation.

When you give attention to that which is good,
you just make more of it.

When man remembers his spiritual connection to All That Is, he lives in a most joyous state wherever he is, whatever he is doing.

*Here are the instructions that we give ourselves
prior to doing our creative work:*

*"I ask that everything needing to be known
is known here today;
I intend that I am guided, guarded, and protected
at all times;
I intend that all of my words
are clear, precise, uplifting, and helpful,
and that they serve the Highest and Best Good
of the Universe, myself, and all beings everywhere.
So be it and so it is."*

What will bring about a mass change of consciousness is enough people thinking and believing and knowing in the Highest Good.

You may have a time when you feel abandoned,
but rest assured that the Highest Good will never abandon you.

Every one of your small, little manifestations is for the Greater Good.

The Highest Good will always send you in the right direction.

*God's plan for you is always
in the Highest and Best Good.
You just have to be willing
to tap into it.*

When you're really listening
and lined up with the Highest Good,
you have to trust that it is in play, that it is happening.

*When you align with people
who are doing things with what you believe,
with what you know to be true,
you're aligning with the Highest Good.*

Your inner guidance is always telling you
to line up with your Highest Good.

The Highest Good has the most beautiful plans
for both you and the world.
You just have to open up to it,
and you do this through silent meditation.

When you see something that's not for your Highest Good,
you know it.
There's no confusion about it.

Our true heroes are the ones
who stand for the Highest Good.

There will be many Earth changes
and they will not be for naught.
They will be for the Highest and Best Good.

If you rely on letting God guide you,
and you rely upon your knowing
that the outcome will be for your Highest and Best Good,
your confusion will fade
and you will become clear.

What you are calling your
Intentions for the Highest Good
are the threads of the cloth being woven
into that which is the robe of peace.

Chapter 10:

UNITY IN COMMUNITY

*The things that you do in your Intenders Circles
and your community gatherings—your group
meditations, stating your intentions and gratitudes and visions for your ideal world, your toning
together, your sharing food—these are helping all
of you to bring balance and unity into your lives.*

—LEE CHING

In our original Intenders Circle, if people needed help, we
helped them. If they were moving, we helped them move.
If they needed some money, we rounded some up for them.
That's the spirit we intended for our community. We helped
each other. We also supported one another in manifesting our
intentions by keeping an eye out for the things that others were
intending to have.

Some of the early manifestations in our first Intenders
Circles got our attention more than others. We'd just gone as
public as you can in Pahoa, Hawaii (which is twenty miles
outside of Hilo), and our Circle was growing fast. On one
particular Sunday evening at our home in Leilani, we had

over thirty people sitting in chairs that ringed the entire living room. Tina started off by intending that she and Mark sell their older white Toyota for a price everyone was happy with. Just as Tina said, "So be it and so it is," our new friends, KaMoi and Mahealani, came in—just in time to hear Tina finish up her intention. Immediately, Mahealani asked if she could see the car. Tina said it was parked downstairs—and long story short—ten minutes later KaMoi and Mahealani bought the white Toyota at a price that made everyone very happy.

You serve yourself well by getting people together
so that they can begin to help each other.
There are groups that are scattered all around,
not knowing that the others even exist.
It is for you to help in bringing them together
so that they know about each other
and each other's good works.
That way, you can help each other
when it comes time to make those stronger stands
for things like peace, equality, freedom, sharing,
and creating a pure, pristine environment for yourselves.

*A community begins
with a few friends getting together.*

*You have come together
for the purpose of waking each other up.*

*Whenever there is a positive group meeting
where you are meeting together and reaching
and searching for that which is a higher life,
there are always those in the higher realms who meet with you,
even though, perhaps, you don't see them.*

Sharing always leads to Oneness.

*A true community is one
where people live life in the moment;
where people help and assist each other
in whatever need arises.*

*It is good to work with someone
who is anticipating the next step.*

Always remind people of their connectedness,
not their separateness.
Look for that which is the same
instead of that which is different.

When your energies are joined together
at an Intenders Circle,
they go up and out. If you could see it—
it is a light that extends up into the heavens—
you would truly be amazed.

When people come together,
peace must be at the core of their intentions,
and then it can be built upon
and something really profound can happen.

In order to have peace,
people must work together.

You mustn't judge, but you must coach.

Be open to people who come toward you,
who are attracted to you.

In the midst of all the strife and craziness,
millions are waking up to the realization
that we are all One.

You cannot deny anymore how the same you are.

In the days ahead,
people will be helping each other and working together
much more than they have in the past.

*Do what you really want in life
and the people who are in alignment with you will show up.*

When your High Self connects with someone else's High Self,
it's absolute magic.

There is magic in your Intenders Circles.
You make good friends, manifest your desires,
and keep each other awake to what you're creating
with your everyday thoughts and words.

Ceremony allows a person to remember who they really are.

Things do not matter as much as people.

The planet is returning more and more
to the communal way of life and family.
It is the action of these communities, not the words,
that will inspire you.

The people who assist you
in going to your next step in life—
those are the people to give freely to.

Surround yourself with people who are supportive
of where you are in your life now.

Separating and dividing yourselves from one another can never lead to Oneness.

Much good comes to you
when you help each other.

Many people have children
they are intending to assist to become
the highest beings they can in this lifetime.

*It is for us in these changing times
to walk the walk and talk the talk
that brings people back to peace and unity.*

Every time you tone together,
the light gets brighter and brighter.

Every community needs its catalysts, its live wires.
It's easy to tell these live wires by their connections.

Ceremony ignites the spark of enthusiasm.
It ignites the light of willpower.
It gives man the strength to carry on.
It gives man the ability to move forward,
to have motivation.

Being part of a community doesn't mean
that everybody is necessarily going to live on the same property.

A typical invocation that we have used in our Intenders Circles:

"We take all of the intentions made here tonight
and we send them out to the Universe
on a pillar of white light
that we create right here in this circle.
We envision this pillar of light going up
through the roof of this house
and reaching out into the heavens above
for as far as we can imagine...
And now we see it going through the floor beneath us,
connecting us to the heart of Mother Earth...
And we see it expanding now,
out past the walls of this building
and across the streets of this community
and all across this land,
inspiring and uplifting everyone it touches.
And now we invite and invoke our guides and helpers.
We call Mother Mary, Jesus Christ, Buddha, Lee Ching,
Kuan Yin, Saint Francis, Krishna, All Our Relations,
The Ascended Masters, The Archangels, Moses, Merlin,
Chief Seattle, White Buffalo Calf Woman, Yogananda,
Gandhi, Saint Germain, [add your own favorite guides],
and all those who stand firm for the Highest Good.
We give great thanks that you join us here today
and we ask that our intentions return to us in great measure.
And, as always, we say that, in order to manifest, all of our
intentions must serve the Highest and Best Good of the
Universe, ourselves, and all others. So be it and so it is."

Sometimes you need the help of a friend
—until you can move mountains again.

Chapter 11:

LETTING GO

Everyone's fear about money is coming to the surface now. The answer lies in trust. Do you trust in your financial portfolio, or in a higher power? A higher power has always been there for you, but you have to trust in it. Indeed, if you look back, you will see that everything you have needed has always come to you. While many are still filled with the fear of not having anything to fall back on, gifts are being given to those of you who are letting go and opening up. It is a great truth that as you surrender, everything shows up.

—LEE CHING

The Intention Process always ends with a letting-go. In our original Intenders Circle, we set out (with Lee Ching's gentle guidance) to learn as much as we could about this process. We intended to put the Law of Attraction to the test, not just talk about it. What we discovered is that there's a point right before things manifested for us—right before we got what we wanted—when we noticed that there is a surrendering, a letting-go, and we found it wise to tell ourselves, "It's okay if I get what I want, and it's okay if I don't get what I want."

We learned that we couldn't allow ourselves to get too attached to the outcome, and that if we held on to our attachment to the outcome beyond a certain point, we'd be sabotaging our intentions and things would begin to get frustrating for us. We had to let go in order to retain our balance and our happiness.

In the long run, we learned that letting go not only plays a big part in the Intention Process; it also plays a big part in all facets of our lives. If we want to be happy, we have to be willing to let go of whatever we are overly attached to.

Here's how Lee Ching put it:

Those who are living in their highest light
know that it is good to share your life and your love—
for we have, indeed, come together for a reason.
Feel free to fill your days and nights with love
for your partner, your family, your friends,
your pets, your possessions, and everything,
for these are all gifts unto you.
Just remember that it is unwise
to let your attachment to anyone or anything
take one minute away from your joy.

The longer you hold on to the old ways,
where one profits at the expense of another,
the longer your challenges will continue.
However, as soon as you let go
and allow Great Spirit to bring about
a solution that is best for everyone,
your challenges will lessen.

When things are breaking in your life—
your possessions, your employment,
your relationships, and so forth—
it's for you to know that new things are on their way to you.

*The only thing that causes suffering
is your attachment to it.*

You're going to learn to trust yourself more and more.

You must raise yourself up and out of grief and drama.
As you align more and more with your Higher Self,
you will become less attached.
You might even find yourself not having strong feelings
over the hurt or death of a family member—
and that is not a bad thing.
It is simply that you have released yourself
from the pressure of the drama
because now you are able to see
that it was their time to move on
or their time for their karma
to be revealed to them.

There are easier ways of doing things.

Things are not happening to you;
they are just happening.

*Some people would rather die
than admit they are wrong.*

Surrender to the fact that you're always taken care of.

The crown chakra (the infant's soft spot at the top of the head) is the tunnel we go through to our next level of consciousness. But first we need to let go.

The body is the servant of the soul.

*Non-attachment to things
leads to non-attachment to the body.*

You have to trust that there is a Higher Power at work in your life and in your world.

People want to go back to the old ways
where it's comfortable—
but we can't do this anymore.

The next step is letting go—not trying to get more.
It's trusting: trusting that your inner guidance
is taking you exactly where you need to go.

The next step beyond intention is surrender.

The more you go toward the Light of God,
the more you surrender—
and the better off you are
in your life and in your death.

You must decide with sincerity,
and then surrender.

You have to be like a cork in the ocean,
letting God take you wherever He wants.

It's good to let go of old things...
so new things can come in and take their place.

Everything gets better when you trust.

Sometimes your best next step is to surrender.

Anger: it happens to all of us.
We should just recognize it.
Don't carry it around
and don't feel guilty because it happened.
It happens to everybody.
Let it go!

In order to have it all,
you've got to give it all up.

How long do you wait?
For as long as it takes.

Fears do you no worldly good.
Let them go.

It is an important part of our growth process that we learn to trust from a very deep level that which we may not have trusted before.

Chapter 12:

LIFTING OFF

Our blessing would be for everyone to become One with each other, One with God, and One with each and every Divine Being [so you can] be able to emulate that which each Divine Being can do—that is, to do the things that Jesus did by being Jesus. It is doing the things that Mother Mary did by inviting the Mother into your heart.

You can begin by opening your hands and making a bowl of your hands. Let Divine Light flow into the bowl, filling you up with beautiful Divine Light. Just open to your Divinity and know that you will be in the right place at the right time, doing whatever is necessary for you to fulfill your Divine purpose. You must be open to find your right place in the world. Everyone has their particular work, their job, their part in the puzzle. So open your hands for Divine Light to flow in. Fill up the bowl, and then place your hands on your heart and bring this Divine Light energy into your being. If you need to think of a certain God or Goddess that you would like to bring into your heart—someone you feel a relationship with—then bring that Being into your heart with you. They will help you from within.

After that, simply open for guidance, and guidance will come in every situation no matter how difficult it is seeming. Focus on your spirituality. Focus on Divine Light until you become it.

—LEE CHING AND KUAN YIN

The Intention Process turns into the Ascension Process. First, however, we have to learn how to create deliberately, consciously—and then we'll have the tools we need in order to become Universal Beings. For that is our destiny in these volatile, shifting times: to transcend our humanity and step out into the bigger Universal picture.

Lee Ching always told us that we are much more than we think we are—that our history is timeless and our Spirit is limitless. In the days to come, he said, we would break out of the cocoons of our small self and start to identify with our Higher Self, the part of us who knows all, sees all, loves all.

This is what awaits us. And this, he said, is when the fun begins.

Indeed, it's clear that many of us are realizing that we made an agreement before we came into these bodies, that we would come together at a certain time in order to bring light and love onto this planet and to usher in a golden age. Some have forgotten, and some just have a feeling, like an inkling of a long-lost dream, that there really is a reason for us to be here now. In either case, on one level or another, we are all experiencing a movement toward looking at life from the perspective of the soul and the soul group—a perspective of having made agreements and arrangements to come here and meet together with other souls and soul groups—and then join together—so that we can assist in raising the vibration of this planet. This is what is being remembered at this time—and it is this movement which will, in fact, bring the golden age into manifestation.

If we want to create a better world for ourselves, we need to start thinking more positively.

*In order for you to go to the next level,
you must unify with your Higher Self,
which sees everything from a higher place,
as if it were a play going on in your life,
as if you were standing atop a mountain
and looking down on it all.*

You will be walking in the footsteps of angels,
for you will be making them yourself.

The world you live in is splitting apart.
The old, selfish ways are collapsing,
and at the same time
the new spiritual ways are emerging,
heralding a better life for all.

You are the bridge to bring Heaven to Earth.

You are becoming your Higher Self.

You are building a light body.
That is what you're here for.

To participate on another level,
you need not know how.
Just know that you want to.

Teleportation will come
as soon as we are a planet at peace.

*Soon there will be so many new Masters
running around and touching everyone
that this world will be a beautiful place to be,
a Heaven on Earth.
It is possible!*

We will create the new reality by Being.
That is all that is required of you.
Just to BE.

The end of the pain merry-go-round
is when you surrender, let go, and fly off.

Awakenings come in stages—
until we get to the Big Awakening.

The people who go to a higher level will save the world.

*You will be leaving the world as you know it
and creating a new one.*

*The light that you carry and the light that you share
are making a whole other layer of Earth.*

The more you open your heart, the more light you bring in,
the more light will be generated to lift the planet.
That's your job.

*The human spirit is crying out for freedom
and it is not to be denied.*

*The best thing you can do is to help yourself
and others into a higher plane of existence.*

All of the changes that are happening
have to happen for us to go to the next level.

You're becoming more...

The more people who awaken,
the more the masses will awaken.

You can go to the next dimension,
or you can stay here and be part of creating Heaven on Earth.

You don't have to die to go to the next dimension.

.

Each challenge is there to guide you
toward the desire of your heart.
Each problem, seen from the positive side,
always turns into a blessing.
Each sorrow leads you to your joy.
Each doubt—to your knowing,
Each lack—to your abundance,
Each debt—to your freedom,
Each feeling of hopelessness—to your power,
Each cry of pain—to your comfort,
Each act of war—to your peace,
Each act of anger—to your love,
And each journey through darkness—
into the light.

*The new perception
is being One with everything and everyone.*

The time of Oneness is coming on.
Start envisioning the Golden Age...

There will be many powers making themselves available to you.

*Nothing stands in the way
of you creating Heaven on Earth,
even now, as we speak.*

It is when we step out of our continuous comfort zone,
when we go above and beyond what is called for,
that we experience our greatness.

It is your birthright to enjoy the experience of Oneness.

It is important for you to know that you are light.
That is what you are.
And even though you don't see that light at all times,
it emanates from within you.

You can have anything and everything
you could possibly dream of—
even a whole new world to live in.

It starts out with a simple thought
that turns into a few spoken words:

"If it be for the Highest and Best Good,
I intend that peace and love and grace
return to this Earth now.
So be it and so it is."

And it ends with all of us,
standing in wonder,
gazing out across the threshold of a new world.

About the Intenders

Over the last twenty years, The Intenders of the Highest Good have put the Law of Attraction (we call it the Intention Process) into practical use, individually and in community groups. This book is the heart and soul of what we learned. Embodied in the Intenders information is a call to take our next step in life, and it provides us with the free tools, in the simplest, most loving way, to live a more awakened daily life (*The Code*), and to create a world that is always in support of us (*The Vision Alignment Project*). It also offers a model for coming together in community (*The Intenders Circle*) that uplifts the individual and the group—and, at the same time, lines everyone up with the Highest Good.

For more information about the Intenders, you can go to
www.intenders.com, www.highestlighthouse.com,
www.intenders.org and www.visionalignmentproject.com.

THE CODE

10 Intentions for a Better World

To have *The Code* work in your life, say it once a day.

THE FIRST INTENT - SUPPORT LIFE
I refrain from opposing or harming anyone. I allow others to have their own experiences.
I see life in all things and honor it as if it were my own. I support life.

THE SECOND INTENT - SEEK TRUTH
I follow my inner compass and discard any beliefs
that are no longer serving me. I go to the source. I seek truth.

THE THIRD INTENT - SET YOUR COURSE
I begin the creative process. I give direction to my life. I set my course.

THE FOURTH INTENT - SIMPLIFY
I let go so there is room for something better to come in. I intend that I am guided, guarded,
protected, and lined up with the Highest Good at all times. I trust and remain open to receive
from both expected and unexpected sources. I simplify.

THE FIFTH INTENT - STAY POSITIVE
I see good, say good, and do good. I accept the gifts from all of my experiences.
I am living in grace and gratitude. I stay positive.

THE SIXTH INTENT - SYNCHRONIZE
After intending and surrendering, I take action by following the opportunities that are
presented to me. I am in the flow where Great Mystery and Miracles abide, fulfilling my
desires and doing what I came here to do. I synchronize.

THE SEVENTH INTENT - SERVE OTHERS
I practice love in action. I always have enough to spare and enough to share.
I am available to help those who need it. I serve others.

THE EIGHTH INTENT - SHINE YOUR LIGHT
I am a magnificent being, awakening to my highest potential. I express myself with joy,
smiling easily and laughing often. I shine my light.

THE NINTH INTENT - SHARE YOUR VISION
I create my ideal world by envisioning it and telling others about it. I share my vision.

THE TENTH INTENT - SYNERGIZE
I see Humanity as One. I enjoy gathering with light-hearted people regularly. When we come
together, we set the stage for Great Oneness to reveal Itself.
We synergize.

Meeting with Lee Ching

As we said previously, Lee Ching is not exclusive to anyone. He will come to you if you are open, stand for the Highest Good, sit quietly, and ask. If, however, you would like to meet with Lee Ching through our Intenders messenger, Tina Stober, you can call Tina in Hawaii at 808-982-6774. Tina works by donation and typically receives $50 to $200 for an hour session. Please be mindful of the time zones so that you call between 9:00 a.m. and 5:00 p.m. Hawaii time.

You can also see Tina and Lee Ching in action in several of our Intenders Channel YouTubes and in all of our Intenders DVDs.

About the Author

TONY BURROUGHS is one of the more prolific visionaries of our time. He is the author of ten self-empowerment books and the cofounder of the worldwide Intenders of the Highest Good community. His widely acclaimed Vision Alignment Project recently surpassed two million alignments. He has produced three full-length DVDs, over 130 YouTube videos for the Intenders Channel and has appeared on numerous TV and radio shows including *Coast to Coast AM*. Tony lives in Pagosa Springs, Colorado.

Photograph by Pagosa Photography.